First published in Great Britain in 1990
PALM TREE PRESS
Rattlesden, Bury St Edmunds,
Suffolk IP30 0SZ

ISBN 0 86208 150 5

Prayer of
Francis of Assisi

Lord, make me an
instrument of your peace:
where there is hatred, let
me sow love:
where there is injury, pardon:
where there is doubt, faith:
where there is darkness, light:
where there is despair, hope,
and where there is
sadness, joy.

Divine Master, grant that I
may not so much seek to
be consoled as to console,
to be understood as to
understand,
to be loved as to love.
For it is in giving that we
receive,
it is in pardoning that we
are pardoned,
and in dying that we are
born to eternal life.

A Prayer for Those Who Live Alone

I live alone, dear Lord,
stay by my side;
in all my daily needs
be thou my guide.
Grant me good health,
for that indeed I pray,
to carry on my work
from day to day.

Keep pure my mind,
my thoughts, my every deed,
let me be kind, unselfish,
in my neighbour's need.

Spare me from fire, from flood,
malicious tongues,
from thieves, from fear,
and evil ones.

If sickness or an accident befall,
then humbly, Lord, I pray,
hear thou my call.
And when I'm feeling low,
or in despair,
lift up my heart
and help me in my prayer.

I live alone, dear Lord,
yet have no fear,
because I feel your presence
ever near.

Amen

I Said A Prayer . . .

I said a prayer for you today
and know God must have heard —
I felt the answer in my heart
although he spoke no word!
I didn't ask for wealth or fame
(I knew you wouldn't mind) —
I asked him to send treasures
of a far more lasting kind!

I asked that he'd be near you
at the start of each new day
to grant you health and blessings
and friends to share your way!
I asked for happiness for you
in all things great and small —
but it was for his loving care
I prayed the most of all!

10

'God Bless You'

How sweetly fall those simple words
upon the human heart;
when friends in holiest terms thus seek
their best wish to impart.
From far or near, they ever seem
to bear a power to cheer you;
and soul responsive beats to soul
in breathing out:
'God Bless You'

The Beatitudes

Blessed are the poor in spirit,
for theirs is the kingdom of heaven.

Blessed are those who mourn,
for they shall be comforted.

Blessed are the meek,
for they shall inherit the earth.

Blessed are those who hunger
and thirst for righteousness,
for they shall be satisfied.

Blessed are the merciful,
for they shall obtain mercy.

Blessed are the pure in heart,
for they shall see God.

Blessed are the peacemakers,
for they shall be called
sons of God.

Blessed are those who are persecuted
for righteousness' sake,
for theirs is the kingdom of heaven.

Matthew 5:3-10

13

Deep Peace . . .

Deep peace of the Running Wave to you.
Deep peace of the Flowing Air to you.
Deep peace of the Quiet Earth to you.
Deep peace of the Shining Stars to you.
Deep peace of the Son of Peace to you.

Celtic Benediction

Friendship

A friend is like a tower strong;
a friend is like the joyous song
that helps us on our way.
When golden ties of friendship bind
the heart to heart, the mind to mind,
how fortunate are we!

For friendship is a noble thing;
it soars past death on angel's wing
into eternity.
God blesses friendship's holy bond
both here and in the great beyond:
a benefit unpriced.

Then may we know that wondrous joy,
that precious ore without alloy;
a friendship based on Christ.

Death Is Nothing At All

Death is nothing at all.
I have only slipped away into the next
room.

I am I, and you are you.
Whatever we were to each other,
that we still are.

Call me by my old familiar name,
speak to me in the easy way
which you always used.

Put no difference in your tone,.
wear no forced air of solemnity or sorrow
Laugh as we always laughed
at the little jokes we
enjoyed together.

Let my name be ever
the household word
that it always was,
let it be spoken without effect,
without the trace of a shadow on it.

Life means all that it ever meant.
It is the same as it ever was;
there is unbroken continuity.

Why should I be out of mind
because I am out of sight?

I am waiting for you,
for an interval,
somewhere very near,
just around the corner.

All is well.

*Henry
Scott Holland*

Do Not Be Afraid

Do not be afraid, for I have redeemed you.
I have called you by your name; you are mine.

When you walk through the waters, I'll be with
you;
You will never sink beneath the waves.

When the fear of loneliness is looming,
then remember I am at your side.

You are mine, O my child, I am your Father,
and I love you with a perfect love.

based on Isaiah 43:1-5

18

A Blessing

May the Lord bless you
and take care of you;

May the Lord be kind
and gracious to you;

May the Lord look on you with favour
and give you peace.

Numbers 6:22-27

The
Twenty-Third Psalm

The Lord is my shepherd,
I shall not want.

He makes me lie down
in green pastures.
He leads me beside still waters;
he restores my soul.

He guides me
in paths of righteousness
for his name's sake.

Even though I walk through
the valley of the
shadow of death,

I fear no evil;
for you are with me;
your rod and
your staff comfort me.

You prepare a table before me
in the presence of my enemies.
You anoint my head with oil.
My cup overflows.

Surely goodness and love
shall follow me
all the days of my life.
And I shall live
in the house of the Lord
for ever.

Prayer of Richard of Chichester

Thanks be to you,
my Lord Jesus Christ,
for all the benefits which
you have given me;
for all the pains and insults
which you have borne for
me,
O most merciful Redeemer,
Friend, and Brother.
May I know you more
clearly,
love you more dearly,
and follow you more
nearly.

Kitchen Prayer

Lord of pots and pans and things,
since I've not time to be
a saint by doing lovely things,
or watching late with thee,
or dreaming in the dawn light,
or storming heaven's gates,
make me a saint by getting meals
and washing up the plates.

Although I must have Martha's
hands,
I have a Mary mind,
and when I black the boots and
shoes thy sandals, Lord, I find.
I think of how they trod the earth,
what time I scrub the floor;
accept this meditation, Lord,
I haven't time for more.

Footprints

One night I had a dream.
I dreamed I was walking along
the beach with
God, and across the sky flashed
scenes from my life. For each scene
I noticed two sets of footprints in
the sand, one belonged to me and
the other to God.

When the last scene of my life
flashed before me I looked back at
the footprints in the sand. I noticed
that at times along the path of life
there was only one set of footprints.

I also noticed that it happened at
the very lowest and saddest times
of my life. This really bothered me

and I questioned God about it.
'God, you said that once I decided
to follow you, you would walk
with me all the way, but I noticed
that during the most troublesome
times in my life there is only one
set of footprints. I don't understand
why in times when I needed you
most, you would leave me.'

God replied, 'My precious, precious
child, I love you and I would never,
never leave you during your times
of trials and suffering. When
you see only one set of
footprints it was then
that I carried you.'

Our Father

Our Father, who art in heaven,
hallowed be thy name.
Thy Kingdom come, thy will be
done,
on earth as it is in heaven.

Give us this day our daily
bread;
and forgive us our trespasses,
as we forgive those who
trespass against us.

And lead us not into
temptation,
but deliver us from evil.

For thine is the Kingdom,
the Power and the Glory,
for ever and ever.

Amen

Take Courage!

I can't change what you're going
through,
I have no words to make a difference,
no answers or solutions
to make things easier for you.

But if it helps in any way,
I want to say I care.

Please know that even when you're
lonely,
you're not alone.

I'll be here,
supporting you with all my thoughts,
cheering for you with all my strength,
praying for you with all my heart.

For whatever you need,
for as long as it takes —

Lean on my love.

27

The Power of Prayer

The day was long, the burden I had
borne seemed heavier than I could
longer bear, and then it lifted — but
I did not know someone had knelt
in prayer; had taken me to God that
very hour, and asked the easing of
the load, and he, in infinite
compassion, had stooped down
and taken it from me.

We cannot tell how often as we
pray for some bewildered one, hurt
and distressed, the answer comes,
but many times those hearts find
sudden peace and rest.
Someone had prayed, and faith, a
reaching hand, took hold of God
and brought him down that day!
So many, many hearts have need
of prayer: Oh, let us pray!

A Promise of Hope

I alone know the plans I have for you,
plans to bring you prosperity and not disaster,
plans to bring about the future you hope for.

Then you will call to me.

You will come and pray to me,
and I will answer you.

You will seek me,
and you will find me
because you will seek me with all your heart.

Jeremiah 29:11-13

The Peace of God

Have no anxiety about anything
but in everything,
by prayer and supplication,
with thanksgiving, let your requests
be made known to God.

And the peace of God,
which passes all understanding,
will keep your hearts and your minds
in Christ Jesus.

Philippians 4:4-7

Take Time

Take time to THINK . . .
it is the source of power.
Take time to PLAY . . .
it is the secret of perpetual youth.
Take time to READ . . .
it is the fountain of wisdom.
Take time to PRAY . . .
it is the greatest power on earth.
Take time to LOVE and BE LOVED. .
it is a God-given privilege.

Take time to BE FRIENDLY . . .
it is the road to happiness.
Take time to LAUGH . . .
it is the music of the soul.
Take time to GIVE . . .
it is too short a day to be selfish.
Take time to WORK . . .
it is the price of success.
Take time to DO CHARITY . . .
it is the key to heaven.

God's Promises

God has not promised
sun without rain,
joy without sorrow,
peace without pain.

But God has promised
strength for the day,
rest from the labour,
light for the way,
grace for the trials,
help from above,
unfailing sympathy,
undying love.

34

When You're Lonely

When you're lonely,
I wish you love.

When you're down,
I wish you joy.

When you're troubled,
I wish you peace.

When things are complicated,
I wish you simple beauty.

When things look empty,
I wish you hope.

35

The Difference

I got up early one morning and
rushed right into the day;
I had so much to accomplish
that I didn't have time to pray.
Problems just tumbled
about me,
and heavier came each task.
'Why doesn't God help me?'
I wondered,
he answered, 'You didn't ask.'

I wanted to see joy and beauty,
but the day toiled on grey
and bleak,

I wondered why God didn't
show me,
He said, 'You didn't seek.'
I tried to come into God's
presence;
I used all my keys at the lock.
God gently and lovingly
chided,
'My child, you didn't knock'.

I woke up early this morning,
and paused before entering
the day;
I had so much to accomplish
that I had to take time to pray.

One Solitary Life

He was born in an obscure village,
the child of a peasant woman.

He grew up in still another village
where he worked in a carpenter's
shop until he was thirty.

He did none of the things one
usually associates with greatness.

He had no credentials but himself.

He was only thirty-three when
public opinion turned against him.

38

He was turned over to his enemies
and was crucified.

When he was dead he was laid in a
borrowed grave.

Nineteen centuries have passed
and today he is the central figure of
the human race.

No one has affected the life of man
on earth as much as that
ONE SOLITARY LIFE.

Prayer for Serenity

God grant me the SERENITY
to accept the things I
cannot change,
COURAGE to change the
things I can,
and WISDOM to know
the difference.

The Lord
Our Protector

I lift up my eyes to the hills.
From whence does my help come?
My help comes from the Lord,
who made heaven and earth.

He will not let your foot be moved,
he who keeps you will not slumber.
Behold, he who keeps Israel
will neither slumber nor sleep.

The Lord is your keeper; the Lord is
your shade on your right hand.
The sun shall not smite you by day,
nor the moon by night.

The Lord will keep you from all evil;
he will keep your life.

The Lord will keep your going out and
your coming in,
from this time forth,
and for evermore.

Ps 121

Paul's Farewell

Be happy
and grow in Christ.

Do what I have said,
and live in harmony and
peace.

May the grace of our Lord
Jesus Christ
be with you all.

May God's love,
and the Holy Spirit's
friendship,
be yours.

2 Corinthians 13:11-14

42

I Am With You Always

I am with you in the springtime
of your life, when joy is new,
And when the summer brings the
fullness of your faith, I'm there
with you.
I am with you in the autumn
of your years, to turn to gold
every memory of your
yesterdays,
to banish winter's cold.
I am with you in the sunshine,
when your world glows warm
and bright.
I am with you when life's
shadows
bring long hours of endless night.
I am with you every moment,
every hour of every day —
Go in peace upon life's journey,
for I'm with you all the way.

43

The Cross in my Pocket

I carry a cross in my pocket;
a simple reminder to me
of the fact that I am a Christian
no matter where I may be.
This little cross is not magic,
nor is it a good luck charm.
It isn't meant to protect me
from every physical harm.
It's not for identification
for all the world to see.
It's simply an understanding
between my Saviour and me.
When I put my hand in my pocket

to bring out a coin or a key,
the cross is there to remind me
of the price he paid for me.
It reminds me, too, to be thankful
for my blessings day by day,
and to strive to serve him better
in all that I do and say.
It's also a daily reminder
of the peace and comfort I share
with all who know my Master
and give themselves to his care.
So, I carry a cross in my pocket
reminding no one but me
that Jesus Christ is the Lord of my life,
if only I'll let him be.

Sympathy

God be with you in your sorrow,
through the night and through the day;
may some blessing come tomorrow that will
clear its cloud away.

God is generous in his giving,
give him now the soul that's fled:
may he bless with
strength the living,
rest eternally the dead.

I Asked Jesus

I asked
JESUS
'How much do
you love me?'
'This much,'
he answered, and
he stretched out
his arms and died.

Be Still

Be still, and know
that I am God

Psalm 46:10

Everything is Possible

This is impossible
for a human being,
but for God
everything is possible.

Matthew 19:26

48